OFFICE OF POPULATION CENSUSES AND SURVEYS

SOCIAL SURVEY DIVISION

A
handbook
for
interviewers

**A manual of Social Survey practice and
procedures on structured interviewing**

Liz McCrossan

London: **HMSO**

Contents

Preface to the third edition

In the years since this handbook was first published there has been a very considerable increase in the level of telephone interviewing and SSD now has a well established Telephone Unit. Computer assisted interviewing is now in use both in the field and in the Telephone Unit for one major survey and is being considered for others. Nevertheless, field interviews carried out by paper and pencil methods continue to be the major interviewing method in SSD. For this reason this handbook continues to address itself to this method although much of what is said will also apply to other modes of interview.

1 The work of Social Survey Division

Social Survey Division (SSD) is part of the Office of Population Censuses and Surveys (OPCS). This government department has a number of functions which include the registration of births, marriages and deaths, the production of population statistics and medical statistics of many kinds, and taking the census of population. SSD is the official social survey organisation within central government and collects information about the circumstances, conditions, behaviour and attitudes of members of the population or parts of it.

The function of social surveys

Government departments require reliable and up-to-date information about events and changes taking place in our society in order to devise appropriate policies and to check whether these are working as intended. The work of Social Survey began in wartime 1941 when the Government needed information about the condition of the population and its morale. Since then the scope of survey activity has grown with the increased complexity of the social and economic policy areas for which government departments are responsible. Social Survey Division carries out surveys on behalf of government departments and the public sector.

Social survey research is part of a wide spectrum of methods and sources by which government is able to keep itself informed about the population. For example, the census of population is conducted every ten years and collects information from each of 18 million households, but the enormous size of the operation severely limits the detail it can provide. Much statistical information is obtained from administrative processes of government linked to the provision of services, employment of staff, and take up of benefits. But often these records cannot tell departments all they need to know.

Social surveys, however, collect information from comparatively small but representative samples of the population. Usually each person selected is interviewed personally by a member of the interviewing staff. This greatly increases the amount and complexity of information that can be gathered. Some of the surveys carried out by SSD are of general population samples but others are of special groups such as mothers of young children, the elderly or the disabled.

Type of survey

The information collected in surveys can be divided into four main types:

1. *Physical condition.* Questions can be asked that provide measures of people's health, their physical handicaps and their need for and use of medical services. In some circumstances surveys also involve the taking of measurements. For example, we have carried out surveys which included dental examinations, the heights and weights of adults, and blood pressure readings.

2. *Behaviour.* Surveys often need to find out about particular aspects of people's behaviour. For example, smoking and drinking habits, infant feeding practices, use of contraception, how people change jobs and homes, are all subjects covered by recent surveys.

3. *Social and economic circumstances.* Most social research needs to classify people into groups according to their social and/or economic position in society. Therefore questions about occupation, education and income are frequently asked. In addition, many surveys concentrate on these important aspects of our lives and investigate in detail such things as housing conditions, access to facilities and services, availability of social support, family structure, sources of income, employment status and history, and patterns of expenditure.

4. *Attitudes and opinions.* In addition to factual questions about people's circumstances and behaviour, surveys can elicit their opinions and attitudes about the particular subject being studied. These often help to explain people's behaviour and are relevant to the kinds of administrative action which may be taken to implement policy changes.

Very often a survey will include questions of all four kinds. For example, the survey of adult dental health involved a dental examination (by a dentist), questions about behaviour in relation to tooth cleaning and visiting dentists, questions to establish social class (as defined by occupation) and access to dental services as well as opinion questions about dentures, tooth loss and experience of going to the dentist.

Surveys carried out by SSD can also be classified in other ways:

1. *Continuous surveys.* Surveys run on a continuous basis and providing quarterly or yearly information to monitor change form a substantial part of the work of SSD. For example, the Family Expenditure Survey is used to show how people's spending habits change over time, how economic policy changes affect incomes, eligibility and take-up of benefits as well as providing weights for

the Retail Price Index. The General Household Survey monitors particular questions in the housing, health, employment, educational and other fields. The National Travel Survey monitors travel patterns. The Labour Force Survey monitors movements in and out of the labour force and provides information about changes in employment status and types of employment. There is also an Omnibus Survey which is used to provide small amounts of information quickly and at short notice.

2. *Repeated surveys.* When continuous collection of information is unnecessary, changes can be monitored by repeating surveys at intervals of, say, two, five or ten years. For example, drinking habits, infant feeding practices, dental health, and school childrens' smoking are monitored in this way.

3. *Ad hoc or once off surveys.* These are surveys which are designed and carried out once to investigate a particular problem or policy area. Here we try to describe the situation and throw light on the way policy may be brought to bear on the issue being investigated.

Role of Social Survey Division

In all these ways SSD provides government with a wide variety of information about people's conditions and how they feel about them. It therefore acts as a bridge between government and the population, making it possible for the public to express their views and for government to keep in touch with the circumstances of the people it governs.

The initiation and conduct of surveys

The surveys carried out by SSD are undertaken at the request of government departments or other public sector bodies who pay SSD for the expenditure involved.

It is the task of SSD to translate a customer's request for assistance into a structured survey which collects the appropriate information and presents the findings in statistical form.

The overall responsibility for surveys is taken by members of the Research Group who act as project managers for one or more surveys. They are responsible for liaison with client departments, the formulation of research proposals, the design and analysis of the survey, for coordinating the work of other branches and for reporting the survey findings. In doing this they work in conjunction with specialist branches who have responsibility on all surveys for their aspect of the work.

The interviewer's role

Because of its functions, SSD must be greatly concerned about the reliability and accuracy of the information it presents to government; the interviewer's role in this is emphasised throughout this handbook and in interviewer training. The interviewer's contribution falls broadly into three areas which are dealt with in subsequent sections of the handbook:

1. *The sample.* For each survey the sample to be interviewed is designed and selected with great care to give an accurate picture of the sector of the population whose circumstances, behaviour or views are the subject of that survey.

    Interviewers need to understand the basic principles of sampling and the importance of following sample instructions precisely (Chapter 2) and of obtaining interviews with as many members of the sample as possible (Chapter 3).

2. *The interview.* The success of the interview in obtaining relevant and accurate information depends firstly on the interviewer's skill in convincing informants of the value of the survey and of the integrity of the interviewer and of SSD (Chapter 3). Secondly, it depends on the appropriate use of the detailed survey questionnaires and understanding of the various types of question which may be included and of the correct ways of handling them (Chapters 4-6).

3. *The findings.* When the completed questionnaires are returned to Headquarters the answers to each question have to be classified and coded so that the information can be analysed, quantified and interpreted. Interviewers need to be sufficiently aware of coding, data editing and computing requirements to appreciate the importance of recording the answers to questions as instructed and of probing for full and precise information.

2 Sampling

The *Sampling Implementation Unit (SIU)* is responsible for selecting the samples on all surveys in accordance with the design instructions of the project manager. The unit is also responsible for the maintenance of sampling frames and the provision of advice on their technical limitations.

Everyone is familiar with the census of population which takes place every ten years. On these occasions every household in the country is visited and information is obtained about each household and its members. The data collected provide figures on the size of the population, the numbers of dwellings and of households and so on. However, because of the huge scale of the task and because each individual has to fill in their own form, for many purposes censuses are neither practical nor the best way of collecting the necessary information. Often a better way of obtaining data about the general population, or a particular section of it, is by means of a *sample survey*. Thus instead of approaching the whole population or group in which we are interested we contact only a representative sample of them.

A sample survey has three main advantages over a census:

1.   It can collect much more detailed information because the data are usually collected in an interview conducted by a trained interviewer.

2.   More direct control can be kept over all aspects of the data collection than is possible with the large scale operation of a census. This means that better quality data can be obtained.

3.   A survey is much less expensive, and therefore, can be carried out more frequently.

However, it is essential that the survey sample is carefully designed so as to represent the population and that interviewers follow sample instructions precisely. It is important that you should become familiar with some of the sampling terminology, how a sample is drawn, and the procedures to be followed by the interviewer.

Population

The population to be sampled need not be all people in the country.

Whilst some surveys do cover the whole of the general population, many surveys are designed to represent only a particular group or section. For example, past surveys have involved postgraduate students, mothers of young babies, and the disabled. Thus the term 'population' is used by samplers to mean the particular group of people of interest for the survey in question.

A random sample

Sampling has many applications in everyday life. For example, samples are taken on a production line to help control quality; when you order wine in a restaurant you taste a little before the rest is poured. You can probably think of many other examples. In such cases, a sample is taken and conclusions are drawn about the whole batch or 'population' from which it came.

The same applies to a sample survey; provided the sample is properly selected from the whole of the relevant population so that it is representative, conclusions can be drawn and applied to the entire population from which the sample was taken.

The aim of sampling then is to obtain a representative sample of the population in question which involves giving each sample unit (person, household,etc) one, and only one, chance of selection.

To do this we usually start with a complete list of the particular population and we then select people or units at regular intervals, that is we do not set out deliberately to include particular ones, for that would introduce bias. By means of such methods, different types of people should appear in the sample in the same proportions as they occur in the population from which they are drawn, for example, if the population contains 50 per cent males and 50 per cent females then the sample should contain about the same proportions.

A sample which is drawn in this way is known as a 'random' or 'probability' sample. However, it must be remembered that it is 'random' in the technical sense that every member of the relevant population has been given an equal chance of selection rather than in the more commonly used sense of being haphazard. Generally speaking, the larger the sample the more likely it is to represent the characteristics of the parent population.

Sample size

Samples also have to be large enough to allow detailed analysis of sub-groups. For example, results may be needed for males and females separately, for different age groups and so on. This means that the sample must be large enough for data about the smallest relevant sub-group to have a high degree of precision.

Estimates based on sample data are subject to a certain margin of error simply because they are based on a sample. However, as long as random sampling methods have been used, this 'sampling error' can be calculated and, in general, the larger the sample the smaller the error and the more precise the estimates.

However, the larger the sample the more expensive the survey so we have to decide upon the smallest sample which will achieve the stated aims. Samples of specific populations may be as low as a few hundred, but are more likely to be in the order of thousands.

Source of a sample

The population to be sampled and the method of selection must be decided upon at the very beginning of a survey.

Before anything else can be done it is necessary to obtain or to draw up a sampling 'frame' from which the units can be selected. Such a frame may exist in the form of a list or map on which every member of the population is included, or it may be necessary to compile a suitable one.

Every member of the population must be included on the frame, otherwise not everyone has a chance of selection and the sample could no longer be said to be representative. It is usually helpful if each member is listed once only since then there is no difficulty in giving everyone the same chance of selection.

General population

When a sample of the general population is required a frequently used frame is the Postcode Address File. This is compiled by the Post Office and lists all addresses to which mail is delivered. Occasionally the electoral register is used. The Postcode Address File is available on computer tape and SSD has its own copy which is updated twice a year. A complete copy of the electoral register is also held by SSD.

The electoral register lists people's names as well as addresses: the names however are not wholly reliable since some of the people will have moved on by the time we call, and there is also a proportion who are omitted altogether from the register. The Postcode Address File has the disadvantage that it includes a considerable number of ineligible addresses, particularly vacant and non-residential addresses. But this is compensated for by the fact that it is more up to date and includes very nearly every address in the country. Since it is available on computer tape a sample from this source can also be drawn more economically than one from other frames.

Specific populations

When a sample is required of a particular group in the population, such as the disabled or college students, we have to find or compile a complete list of all members of the group. The same criteria apply here as above, namely that every member of the population must be included, but included only once, in the frame.

In many cases these lists are confidential and the sample has to be drawn to our instructions by the holder of the list who also gives the selected individuals an opportunity to be deleted from it. In other cases we compile our own list by writing to a very large sample of the general population and asking them to complete a short 'screening' question-naire.

Drawing a sample

The procedures followed in drawing a sample can become quite complex. We outline them here in order to demonstrate the care that must be taken to ensure the greatest possible accuracy and so that you have an under-standing of the principles of drawing a sample and can explain to potential informants how they came to be selected.

Single stage sampling

In theory the simplest way of selecting a representative sample of adults in Great Britain would be to take a list of them, such as the electoral register, and choose names at a constant interval throughout.

However, such a sample would pose problems for interviewers because informants would be widely scattered throughout the country and it would result in large costs for locating the sample, travelling and so on.

We are therefore left with two competing needs:

1.   To obtain a representative sample of the population by means of random selection.

2.   To avoid the need for each interviewer to travel widely.

The way in which this is resolved is by using a 'multi-stage' or 'clustered' sampling design.

Multi-stage sampling

In 'two-stage' sampling we:

1.   Select a random sample of 'primary sampling units' (PSUs) or areas.

2.   Draw a random sample of people or addresses within these, rather than across the whole population.

Thus, the first stage in designing a multi-stage national sample is to select a representative sample of areas. Various types of units are used as PSUs but, regardless of the unit used, the same principles apply.

Probably the most frequently used units are postcode sectors. These contain an average of just over 2,500 addresses. These sectors vary in many respects, and to ensure that the sample will be representative we first divide them into several groups:

1.   Often the first grouping is a geographic one into regions of the country with a sub-division between metropolitan and non-metropolitan. The sample of sectors can then be selected in such a way that it is correctly distributed geographically throughout the country and we will not by chance pick too many sectors from, say, the south of the country or from rural areas.

The next procedure is usually to sub-divide these groups of sectors still further and the way in which this is done depends on the subject matter of the survey. Factors commonly used for this purpose are: population density, the proportion of the population in particular socio-economic groups and the proportion of council tenants.

This process of grouping sectors (or other units) is known as 'stratification'. The aim in all stratification is to group together those units which are most similar in some way. Then, by making sure that our sample of sectors is distributed between the groups in the same proportions as the population, we can be more certain that it will represent the characteristics of all districts in the country than if we selected the primary units by simple random method.

2.   The second stage in drawing a sample is that of selecting addresses from within the chosen areas. It is easiest to demonstrate how this is done by looking at an example:

Suppose 20 addresses are required from a sector containing an estimated 2,400. The interval at which they should be selected is calculated by dividing the total number of addresses by the sample size, that is:

$$\frac{2,400}{20} = 120$$

This means that we should select every 120th address.

We do not know where on the list to begin as the starting point could be any one up to and including the 120th. We use the computer to generate a random number between 1 and 120 so that we are equally likely to start with 1, 2 ... 119, 120 and thus we can be sure that everyone in the population has had an equal chance of selection.

Having followed these procedures we have drawn a representative random sample which is distributed in such a way as to be practical and economical for the interviewer.

Whom to interview

Depending on the subject matter of the survey the units of interest may be individuals or households. The sampled units which are issued to interviewers are usually addresses but sometimes are individuals and these have different implications for what the interviewers must do.

Individuals: named persons sample

Such a sample can be one of individuals either within the general population or within a special population, for example, elderly people or mothers of young babies.

Named individuals are selected and it is these people and no others who must be interviewed. For example, if you are told to interview Mary Jones at 35 Rochester Way and you arrive to find that she no longer lives there you must try to discover her new address so that she can be interviewed.

Address sample

Addresses as given on the Postcode Address File usually contain only one household but may contain more. These are called multi-household addresses. If the units of interest for a particular survey are households then, since the Postcode Address File only lists addresses, it is up to the interviewer to carry out the final stage of sampling households within addresses where necessary. In fact there are very few multi-household addresses and these occur predominantly in London and the Scottish cities. If the units of interest to the survey are individuals and the sample issued is one of addresses you will be given instructions on how to select an individual or individuals for each selected address.

All samples

The difference between an address sample and a named person sample is that in an address sample the people or households to interview are those who are living at the address when you first call. In a named person sample the address is only of secondary importance and it is the named person who should be seen.

You should never substitute another individual or address for one which has been sampled because this will mean that members of the population no longer have the correct chance of selection.

Substitution can lead to bias in the results; for example, on an employment survey a worker who is very difficult to contact because of his long working hours may have very different views and concerns from one who is home by 5.00 pm every day. If you substituted one for the other this would lead to bias in the results. The danger of bias is always present no matter how alike two people seem in their external characteristics.

The interviewer's role as sampler

1. For some surveys where we need to interview particular sections of the population for which no lists are available, the easiest way of reaching them may be for interviewers to call at a large number of addresses to find out whether any occupants belong to the relevant groups. Interviews are then carried out only at the addresses containing the eligible people. When this kind of 'sift' as it is called is required, the interviewer has the task of identifying the sample before the usual work of interviewing can begin.

2. On some occasions we rely on the interviewer to draw some units of the sample. For example, you may be asked to select a sub-sample of individuals at an address, or a household at a multi-household address. When this is the case, you will be given special instructions.

3. Occasionally interviewers are asked to carry out the complete task of drawing a sample locally because there is no central source available. Examples of this are prisons or residential homes where a sample has to be drawn within each institution.

As the details above demonstrate, a lot of care is involved in designing a statistically valid sample. As an interviewer it is up to you to ensure that this sample is correctly identified and interviewed.

We have described the way in which a sample is drawn so that you can explain to the public how they came to be selected, the methods by which the process was carried out, and hence the importance of their cooperation. You must make it clear that we can only obtain an accurate cross-section of the population in our sample if the random selection procedures are adhered to and if people are willing to cooperate. You can explain to your potential informants why you need to speak with them and cannot, for example, call next door instead.

Contacting addresses

Although we give you considerable information on address lists there may be more which would help you locate your address. If you have any difficulty in finding an address there are several sources which may be helpful: examples of such sources are the local Post Office or sorting office, the police, and local shopkeepers. The Sampling Implementation Unit may also be able to provide additional information: for example, the Unit holds a complete set of electoral registers which will usually help to pinpoint an address and will supply a name which can be helpful in rural areas.

The telephone number of the person to contact in such cases, or with any other sampling query, is included in the interviewer instructions for each survey.

3 Approaching the public

Initial contact between interviewer and informant

The success of the work of Social Survey Division depends on the goodwill of the general public and on their willingness to cooperate in surveys voluntarily. No one is compelled to give an interview. The number of people who are willing to cooperate in surveys and the quality of the information they provide depends very much on the way in which you, the interviewer, approach them and on how well you explain the purpose of the enquiry.

In advance of your call SSD will have written to each sampled address to let them know of your visit and the survey for which they have been selected. In most cases the person you encounter will have seen the letter and will remember it but you must be prepared for this not to be so. Whatever the situation you must work quickly to establish rapport with a stranger and to persuade him that our survey is worth while. It is generally advisable to keep your initial introduction brief as you will not normally have been invited in at this stage. Briefness is particularly advisable if you are talking to only one person when you wish to interview the whole household or if you are talking to someone other than your named informant. If you are talking to the chosen person and he/she is immediately cooperative, you must let them know approximately how long the interview takes before starting on it. Many people will assume that it will only take 10 minutes or so and may wish to make an appointment rather than talk to you there and then when they realise that it will take much longer than this (most of our interviews take about 1 hour).

If your informant is less immediately cooperative, try to make an appointment to explain the purpose of the survey more fully, making it clear that you are not necessarily assuming that you can interview them. If someone is being evasive or disinterested, this is often preferable to trying to persuade him there and then: and if you are trying to talk to several members of a household it becomes very important to try to see and explain to them all.

You must always try to judge the best way to react to your informant in order to gain his cooperation.

If you are talking to someone other than your named informant, it is best to say as little as possible about the purpose of your call. But remember that you can easily arouse suspicion and that it is therefore advisable if talking to a close relative to explain who you are working for and to show your authorisation card. Survey explanations passed on through a third party often get distorted and it is for this reason we suggest that you avoid giving details to anyone other than your informant.

Whoever you meet when you first make contact at an address you should be alert for any sign that your call has been made at an inconvenient time. Screaming children, shouting in the background, a long delay in answering the door may all be signs that you have called at an inconvenient time: if this happens it is best to apologise and withdraw gracefully saying that you will call again.

At your first visit to an address you should always briefly show your authorisation card whether or not you are asked for it.

Unless we have instructed you otherwise you must not write or telephone for an appointment with your informant. Initial contact should be made in person.

Gaining cooperation

Although we suggest that doorstep contact should be brief you must be prepared if necessary to argue the case for your survey on the spot; and of course when returning to keep an appointment you should be prepared, not just to explain, but also to convince a reluctant informant. In doing this there are several useful lines which you can follow. Irrespective of the subject matter of any particular study it is always possible to explain that surveys are valuable as a means of providing government with information which they cannot get from other sources. A survey can provide an up-to-date picture of some aspects of the way of life of members of the public or show their reactions to any national issue. Our findings can help decide a future policy matter or help a Department judge the effects of past policy. Some information about past surveys we have done is given in Chapter 1 of this handbook and also in a general leaflet with copies of which you will be issued. In addition to this every survey you work on provides you with more information. Surveys provide good information on which government can plan its services and also act as a way of keeping in touch with what public needs and ideas really are. This idea appeals to many people, and is often a good approach to adopt.

In addition to these general points you will have been given as much information as possible about the purposes of the survey on which you are working at the time.

You should always know why the information is considered important and what problems the survey is designed to study. With this information, before starting work on any survey, you will need to think out several ways of introducing it to the public. You may be able to emphasise different facets of the survey purpose to suit different types of people. Adolescents, housewives, professional and retired people would not all respond equally well to precisely the same introduction. Some interviewers find it helpful to practise introductions with the aid of a tape recorder.

Whenever you approach an informant it is up to you to judge his reactions to your explanations and to change tack if necessary.

There are one or two common reactions which you need to be prepared to cope with. Some people will insist that they are not typical: in this case you must explain that the survey is not accurate if it does not show how many people are atypical and in what ways they are atypical. Others will say that they know nothing about the subject matter of the survey and will genuinely feel that they would be of no use: in this case you must persuade them that everyone is of importance and that the survey findings are distorted if only people who know a great deal about the subject are interviewed. Many people will react by suggesting that you interview someone else. Often this is combined with feeling atypical or lacking in knowledge and in these cases, as well as making the points outlined above, you need to explain the way in which the sample is drawn and the importance of getting a cross-section of people. All this may sound daunting when you have never tried it, but with a little practice these arguments will come very readily to you.

Essential introductory points

Before beginning an interview with an informant there are a number of points which we think it essential that you make to him. Some of them at least you will almost certainly have covered on the doorstep, but in such cases it is usually wise to repeat them again inside the house as at the doorstep stage informants are often paying only limited attention to exactly what you are saying.

The points which you must cover are:

1.   The name of our organisation.

2.   The name of the department(s) on whose behalf the survey is being undertaken.

3.   An explanation of how the person/household came to be selected for the survey.

4.   The purpose of the survey and/or the uses to which the information will be put.

5. The confidential nature of the enquiry: the identity of informants is not disclosed to any other government department, nor to members of the public or press, nor to anyone who is not an authorised representative of OPCS. All survey findings are presented in such a way that no individual informant can be identified.

6. The voluntary nature of their cooperation: this does not necessitate the use of the actual word 'voluntary' and is often covered by saying 'Would you be willing to help us?' You must of course be quite explicit if an informant asks you whether or not a survey is voluntary.

You must also show households/informants your authorisation card and make sure that they have sufficient time to give you before commencing the interview.

When you first begin work you may find it helpful to attach a single-word reminder list of these points to your clipboard but you should try to memorise the list before starting work.

Identifying the correct person or household

In the majority of cases this is very simple but on some types of sample there are slightly more complex procedures to be followed. The first thing to ensure is that you are calling at the correct address: this can usually be done by exercising care with street names and house numbers or names, but on occasion you may have to check that you are at the correct address when you first speak to someone there. Thereafter for a named person sample you should give the name in as much detail as you have it. You will normally know the sex (but not the marital status) and either the full Christian names or initials. In virtually all cases this will identify your informant clearly. Occasionally you may come across, for example, a father and son with the same name: often the purpose of the survey and source of the sample will enable you to know which of two people you want to talk to. In any cases of doubt you must refer to HQ for guidance.

When trying to contact a whole household you need to explain the household definition (see p 49) and establish who are the people who fall within it. On many surveys we instruct you or advise you to make an appointment to call when you can explain the survey to all these people together: on others we may give you more leeway and let you interview informants as you find them at home. The decision as to which way to deal with an individual survey is made according to how essential it is to have the cooperation of everyone and on the extent to which we think a single interview can prejudice the cooperation of other household members. Even when you are allowed to interview individuals as you meet them, it is often unwise to carry out your first interview with a secondary member of the household such as a young son or the daughter or an elderly mother.

Doorstep sifts

On occasion you will be asked to identify and interview a particular 'role' member in a household, usually the householder, that is, the person in whose name the house is owned or rented. At other times surveys demand that you list all the people resident in a household and then either interview anyone in, for example, a particular age group or employment situation or follow a sampling procedure to select one individual only. Wherever 'sifts' of this kind are required you are given detailed instructions in a survey briefing.

Whenever you are asked to carry out a sift, or identify a role member, you should introduce yourself as from Social Survey, explain that you have been asked to call at the address but that you are uncertain who you wish to see, or if you wish to see anyone, until you have asked one or two simple questions. In these situations it is particularly important to remember to show your authorisation card on the doorstep.

Non-response

On any survey the proportion of informants who have cooperated in it is one of the most important measures of the validity and accuracy of the survey findings. Without a high level of cooperation concern arises as to whether those who refused were different in some important respect from those who cooperated. This, in turn, throws a doubt on the representativeness of the sample.

As an interviewer there are three types of non-response you will come across.

1. *Ineligible informants.* There are some addresses/people which are ineligible on all surveys. These are:

   (a) demolished or empty addresses (on an address sample);

   (b) addresses which are used only on an occasional basis, for example, a holiday home or a weekday pied a terre;

   (c) named individuals who have died; and

   (d) named individuals who have emigrated, that is, gone to live (semi) permanently in a foreign country.

In addition, on particular surveys, other types of addresses or people may be defined as ineligible because they do not form part of the relevant survey population. On an employment survey, for example, households where everyone is 65 or over may be defined as ineligible.

Non-response of this type is normally excluded when cooperation rates are quoted and does not adversely affect the findings of the survey since the individual or address concerned is not within the population which the sample is intended to represent.

2.   *Refusals.* These can come direct from a selected informant or household or from one member of a household speaking on behalf of himself and/or other household members, or may arise from evasion or failure to keep appointments. In all cases you must do your best to obtain cooperation not only by explaining the survey but also by calling back again when an appointment is broken or someone is evasive. Remember, however, that the public is free to refuse to be interviewed and that it is wrong to persist in calling when they have clearly shown that they are unwilling to cooperate.

When you have had a refusal or refusals try not to let it lower your morale in such a way that your dejection and lack of confidence show to other people as you call on them. This could easily precipitate another refusal.

After a refusal it is often helpful to think through the circumstances and the approach you employed. There are a number of questions which you can ask yourself:

(a)   Were you dressed in any way unsuitably for the area?

(b)   Were you calling at an unconventional time for the area, for example, too late in the evening?

(c)   Were there any indications, which you missed or ignored, that the time of your call was awkward for your informant, for example, was he clearly just going out or about to have a meal?

(d)   Was there anything inappropriate in the way in which you introduced yourself and explained the survey?

(e)   Did you react sensibly and quickly to his attitude and to the ideas which he expressed?

By thinking about such questions you can build gradually but surely on your own experience.

You will be notified of any refusal made direct to HQ as a result of an advance letter and these will not be counted as your non-response.

3. *Non-contacts.* A number of different situations are included in this category. On a household sample, however, any address at which you have seen any member of the household should be shown as a refusal. Non-contacts include the following:

(a) Informants who are away from home throughout the fieldwork period, for example, in hospital or prison or on an extended holiday.

(b) Named informants who have moved and whose new address you are unable to trace.

(c) Households or individuals whom you have never been able to find at home.

All these cases are included as non-response because they represent a real loss to the sample and the data, but clearly some of them are purely circumstantial and cannot be controlled by you in any way. To minimise non-contacts you should call at all addresses in your quota early in the fieldwork period so as to avoid missing people who will be away later. You should also make several calls at different times and in different weeks at addresses where you are having difficulty in contacting someone. After one or two calls at an address you should try contacting someone at an adjacent house as a neighbour can often provide useful information about the times when someone is normally at home; as with other members of the informant's household, it is advisable when talking to neighbours to show your authorisation card and explain who it is you are working for.

Our general ruling on the number of calls required is that at least 4 should be made when trying to establish contact and that at least 2 of these calls should be in the evening or on Saturday.

For all non-response we ask you to code the reason for refusal or non-contact.

Other points about contacting informants

Appointments

It is most important to keep any appointment which you make with a member of the public: a semi-appointment should also be regarded as binding on your part.

If for any reason you find yourself unable to keep an appointment you should call or write in advance to cancel it if this is possible. If this is not possible you should ring your Region who will try to arrange for another interviewer to keep your appointments.

Resident employees

If your informant proves to be an employee, such as a maid or housekeeper, who lives in the employer's home, you must establish that the employer is willing for the employee to be interviewed. You should also however make it clear to the employee that his cooperation is voluntary.

Minors

On either a named person or a household survey, if your informant is under 16 years of age and living in the parental home the permission of one or other parent (or guardian) should be obtained before the interview takes place.

Letters

As a last resort you may find it useful to leave a personally written letter at an address where you have had difficulty in making contact or hope to persuade them to change their mind about refusing. Your are provided with example letters, message cards, and headed notepaper.

General behaviour

You should never tell anybody else the name of anyone you have interviewed on our behalf nor anything which is said in the course of an interview or any other contact with an informant. No other informant or household should know who else has been selected. Both completed and blank questionnaires should be looked after carefully and even blank questionnaires should never be given to members of the public or left with informants. Neither questionnaires or address lists should be left lying around in public view, for example, loose in your car.

Should you ever find yourself involved in a general discussion about survey work you should confine yourself to talking about continuous surveys and surveys which have been completed. You must never discuss the work of Social Survey or of OPCS with any member of the press. Any reporter who shows an interest in our/your work should be referred to the Press Office at HQ.

In all dealings with informants, their families, members of the public and officials of any kind you should behave in a responsible and businesslike way and must never allow your personal feelings to influence your behaviour.

Your authorisation card should also be looked after very carefully and if at any time you are unfortunate enough to lose it you must make every endeavour to recover it. You should also immediately inform both the local police and Field Branch of its loss.

4 Questionnaires and types of questions

The interviews that are carried out by Social Survey Division are all highly structured. This means that all the questions you ask of informants are printed word for word as they should be asked and are arranged in a particular order in a printed schedule or questionnaire. This ensures that all informants are asked the same questions in the same sequence. Similarly the ways in which you are required to record answers on the printed schedule are standardised. This ensures firstly that answers to the same question from different informants are recorded in a comparable way and, secondly, that the process of transferring the answers from the schedule to the computer is as efficient as possible. In the end all answers to questions are reduced to a number or set of numbers. Much of this is achieved by the methods you use to record the answers at the interview. The rest is done by clerical staff in the office.

The aim of this chapter of the handbook is to enable you to identify the main types of questions and to become familiar with the format of questionnaires.

The questionnaires used at the main field work stage of surveys are the result of several weeks or months of preparatory work. They will have been tested by means of a pilot survey before the mainstage is launched and the final design and layout is therefore the result of careful thought and experiment.

Question filters and dependent questions

It is very unusual to have a questionnaire in which all questions are asked of all informants. Instructions on the sequence of questioning which you should follow are known as 'filter' instructions and are shown on questionnaires in two main ways.

The most straightforward and commonly used filter instruction is printed beside the list of answers and tells you which question you should ask next according to the answer you have been given. It may direct you either to a later main question or to a subsidiary part of the question you have just asked: such subsidiaries are normally described as *dependent questions*. The second type of instruction is printed as a heading above a particular question or group of questions and refers you back to the answers given at one or more previous questions. Headings of this type are used when the sequence of questions cannot follow directly from the answer to any preceding question and normally define the categories of informant of whom the questions should be asked. They are often accompanied by a DNA (does not apply) code to give you further instructions.

The example given below shows both types of instruction. The heading tells you which groups of people should be asked the question, the instructions against the DNA code and the possible answers direct you to the next question which may need to be asked.

TO ALL MARRIEDS, WIDOWED, DIVORCED OR SEPARATED AND TO SINGLES LIVING AS MAN AND WIFE (CODED 1 AT Q.13)

DNA, OTHER SINGLES   X—See Q.17

| Have you any step, foster, or adopted children who live with you | | Yes .... 1 ASK (A)
No .... 2 SEE Q.17 | | | |

IF YES

(a) ENTER DETAILS BELOW:

		1st child	2nd child	3rd child	4th child
	step	1	1	1	1
	foster	2	2	2	2
	adopted	3	3	3	3
date of birth:	month	....	....	....	....
	year	....	....	....	....
date started living with informant:	month	....	....	....	....
	year	....	....	....	....

The example given here is very simple and many schedule filters demand much more careful scrutiny than does this one.

One particular point to note is that 'ASK Q....' is used when that question is definitely applicable, 'SEE Q...', as here, is used when the question to which you are directed contains an additional instruction and will not need to be asked in all cases.

Ways of asking questions

Questionnaires contain many different styles of questioning, all of which demand different interviewing techniques and different ways of recording the answers.

By presenting the questions to informants in different ways it is possible to vary the amount and type of information collected. A compromise is almost always necessary between letting the informant answer in the form which comes most naturally to him and imposing a response framework which makes it easier to compare the answers of different informants.

As an interviewer you need to be familiar with all question types.

Open questions

An open question is one which requires the informant to answer the question in his or her own words. It differs from other question types in that the wording of the question does not restrict the way in which the informant may answer.

1.   Why did you go to live away from your parents?

2.   Can you tell me why you approve of sex before marriage?

In these two cases the purpose of the question was to explore fully informants' reasons and views. A large space was left on the questionnaire and the interviewer probed for a full answer which she recorded verbatim.

Answers to open questions are time consuming for the interviewer to record and also time consuming to deal with in the office. For these reasons an open question sometimes has *codes* listed on the questionnaire for the interviewer to code. A *code* is simply a number used to identify a particular category of response.

This type of question is known as a *'precoded open question'*.

Why did you stop work?	Pregnancy/to start a family	1
PROBE FULLY	To get married/change of domestic responsibilities	2
	Own ill health/accident	3
	Retired - PROBE whether voluntary	4
	or compulsory....	5
	Redundancy/job finished	6
	Other (SPECIFY)	11
	....	
	....	

You will see that there is an instruction at the question to *probe fully*. This is to remind you that the purpose of such open questions is to explore fully the informant's thinking. Interviewer coding of open questions is only worthwhile when the answers to the question tend to be straight-forward and when experience tells us that most answers can be easily assigned to one of the precode categories.

Precoded open questions are frequently used to collect quantitative information such as times and distances.

Was your husband/fiance unemployed at all during that period?	Yes .... 1 ASK (a)	
	No 2	

(a)   For how long altogether was he unemployed during that time?

Less than 4 weeks	1
One month but less than 3 months	2
3 months but less than 6 months	3
1 year or more	4
Don't know/can't say	5

Unlike the previous example, open questions of this kind do give the informant an indication of the form of the answer expected. In this case *'For how long altogether was he unemployed during that time?'* tells the informant that a length of time is required.

Sometimes although the form of the question is kept open, the technique of using precodes is taken a step further and a range of precodes is printed on a card which is given to the informant to suggest some likely answers to them (see example below). If the question is of a personal

What are your reasons for starting work again?		
	Working is the normal thing to do	1
HAND CARD C		
	Need money for basic essentials such as food, rent or mortgage	2
CODE ALL	To earn money to buy extras	3
THAT APPLY	To earn money of my own	4
	For the company of other people	5
	Enjoy working	6
	To follow my career	7
	Other reasons (SPECIFY)	8

nature the informant may answer by giving only the code no(s) of item(s) on the card. The question remains open both because alternatives are not suggested in the wording itself and because answers other than those on the card are equally acceptable. In these cases the card basically functions as a check list only.

Since marriage have you and
your husband used any of these
methods to prevent you becoming pregnant?

SHOW CARD B   Yes ..... 1 ASK a
                                               No   ...... 2 GO TO Q100
_____

    a.   Which methods have you used?

    1.   Withdrawal (the man is careful and pulls out before climax)

    2.   Sheath, condom, Durex, French letter

    3.   The pill

    4.   Diaphragm, cap or Dutch cap

    5.   Coil, loop or intrauterine device

    6.   Chemicals, spermicides, 'C' film

    7   Rhythm or Safe Period

    8.   Female sterilisation, tubes tied or male sterilisation, vasectomy

    9.   Abstain (not having sex for several months to avoid getting pregnant)

    10.   Any other method

As with ordinary precoded opinion questions this technique is only possible if the likely answers to the question fall into a number of clearly identifiable categories.

In the example shown above, the card has several purposes. The card is handed to the informant to help her answer the main part of the question. First it shows her which methods are regarded as methods of contraception for the purpose of the survey. This helps the informant give a precise yes or no answer to the main part of the question. At the open part (a) of the question the card allows the informant to answer with a number rather than a word if she is embarrassed or is not alone during the interview. In this example the card was used for clarification and ease of question asking and answering rather than to precode the answers.

Closed or forced choice questions

All the types of questions of which you have seen examples so far are open questions because the informant is not *required* to answer within a restricted range of choices, even when a range of possible answers is offered. As soon as the wording of the question demands that a choice is made from a range of set answers the question becomes a *closed* or *forced choice* question and the interviewer's main task is to ensure that the question is answered in the set terms only.

In the simplest type of forced choice question the choice is only implicit and the question requires simply a *yes/no* answer (see box below, example a.).

---

a. Have you used a vehicle for business/work
purposes in the last three months?

Yes	.....	1
No	.....	2

b. Are there any unoccupied flats or
bedsitters in this house/building?

Yes	.....	1
No	.....	2
Don't know	.....	3

c. Now thinking about abortion - if you
found you were pregnant when you
did not want to be, would you want to
have an abortion or not?

Yes	..	1)	
Qualified (SPECIFY)		2)	ASK(a)
No	...	3	

The second of these examples (see b.) shows that there are some questions where the researcher is aware that not all informants will know the answer. 'Don't know' (often shortened to DK) is therefore a legitimate answer and a precode is provided for it. The third example illustrates the use of a qualified answer in a *yes/no* question. These codes are included only when the pilot has shown that a minority of informants will insist on adding a qualification to their answer. In response to this question, for example, many informants gave answers related to their health or the health of the baby.

Usually an answer which is qualified has to be recorded in full but occasionally only the ringing of the code is required.

The main way in which a forced choice question is used is in cases where the research officer wishes to present the informant with alternative answers (see box top opposite).

IF WORKING 12 MONTHS AGO

At that time, 12 months ago, were you:

working as an employee	1)	Q.25A/B
or were you self-employed? ...	2)	PAGE 12

When you first leave home (I mean before you get
married) do you think you will be buying or renting
your accommodation?

Buying	1	GO TO Q61
Renting	2)	
Not sure/it depends	3)	ASK (a) & (b)
Other (SPECIFY)	4	GO TO Q60

Running prompts

The closed question format just described is appropriate when the informant is presented with only two choices. Whenever the number of choices to be given is greater than this the question is laid out differently and is known as a *running prompt*. However, both the way in which you are expected to handled the question and the way in which the informant is expected to answer are identical, that is, you must read out the whole of the question down to the question mark.

Can I just check, when you left hospital
were you ....

bottle feeding completely	1	GO TO Q81
RUNNING breast feeding completely	2)	
PROMPT or giving both bottle and breast...	3)	ASK (a)

How satisfied were you with the help and advice
about feeding you received in hospital?

On the whole were you .. very satisfied	1	SEE Q75
fairly satisfied	2)	
RUNNING rather dissatisfied	3)	ASK (a)
PROMPT or very dissatisfied	4)	

DO NOT PROMPT Received no help or advice......	5	ASK (b)

The above question enables us to place each informant on a four-point scale measuring her satisfaction with help and advice received in hospital. The question has an extra code for the small number of informants who spontaneously answered that they had received no help or advice. You are reminded not to read this answer as part of the question by the instruction *do not prompt*. This instruction is sometimes phrased as *spontaneous only*.

Card prompts

On some occasions, rather than reading out all the categories of a running prompt, the possible answers are printed on a card which is shown to the informant. This happens particularly when the same running prompt is used for several different questions on the schedule.

Now I should like to ask you how you feel about your present (main) job, and the answers I should like you to choose from are printed on this card.

SHOW CARD B

(a) How satisfied are you with
  your job as a whole?

Very satisfied	1
Fairly satisfied	2
Neither satisfied nor dissatisfied	3
A little dissatisfied	4
Very dissatisfied	5

Individual prompts

Sometimes a forced choice question is laid out as a single question but includes a list of items about each of which an answer is required. This is known as an *individual prompt*.

After the baby was born did you have any extra help around the house or with the baby, from ....

		Yes	No
	Your husband?	1	x
	Other relatives?	2	x
INDIVIDUAL PROMPT	Friends or neighbours?	3	x
	A home help?	4	x
	None of these?	5	x

As can be seen the question is first asked about 'your husband' then about 'other relatives' and so on. Only if 'no' is recorded at each of the four types of help is the fifth check category 'none of these?' asked.

Scaling questions

An extended version of this technique is used when a series of questions requiring answers on a scale is needed. In this case the list of *items* is treated as an *individual prompt*. The range of possible *answers* takes the form

28

of a *running prompt* which is often printed as a card because it is used repeatedly. Questions of this type are usually referred to as *scaling questions*.

Could I ask you now how useful you think methods of looking for work are/would be for you personally (if you had to find a job). Can you choose your answers from this card.				
HAND CARD E	Very useful	Fairly useful	Not very useful	DK
What about				
(a) Asking around people you know? ...	1	2	3	4
(b) Approaching employers directly? ...	1	2	3	4
(c) Using the government Employment Office or Jobcentre?	1	2	3	4
(d) Looking at advertisements?	1	2	3	4
(e) Using private employment agencies?	1	2	3	4

In the above example there are five similar questions requiring answers from the same 'usefulness' scale.

Priority coded prompts

In all these closed or prompted questions it has been essential to present the informant with the complete range of choices open to him. There is, however, one type of prompt which is an exception to this rule. These are known as *priority coded prompts* and are used when more than one code can apply and the list of codes has been arranged in order of descending importance. These questions are marked 'code first that applies' and it is not necessary to prompt the categories which follow a positive answer.

Apart from leisure classes, and ignoring holidays, are you at present:		
CODE	at college or university full-time?	1
	on a sandwich course?	2
FIRST	training for a qualification in nursing, physiotherapy, or similar medical subject?	3
THAT	at college part-time on day or block release?	4
APPLIES	Doing an Open University course?	5
	NONE OF THESE?	6

The types of questions illustrated so far are those which you will come across most frequently: you will probably find examples of all of them on any questionnaire. In addition to these however there are a considerable number of other question types, some of which occur frequently enough for it to be worthwhile to include examples of them in this handbook.

Rank ordering questions

This is another technique for measuring informants' views on a scale the aim of which is to obtain direct comparisons between a number of items. This is done by asking the informant to arrange the items on a set of cards in order of importance or some similar concept.

I would like to find out how you would compare total deafness with other handicaps or disabilities. Would you arrange these cards in order, starting with the most severe handicap or disability, down to the least severe?

SHUFFLE WHITE CARDS AND HAND
TO INFORMANT
INTERVIEWER CODE AND RECORD

RANK

RANKS -

MOST SEVERE = 1

LEAST SEVERE = 6

	RANK
total deafness	....
blindness	....
epilepsy	....
confined to a wheelchair	....
losing a leg	....
having a heart condition	....

Self completion questions

When a scaling question is used which includes an unusually lengthy list of items it is often simpler and quicker to have the informant record the answers himself in the course of the interview. There are several different ways in which these questions can be laid out and they are usually printed on a separate sheet from the rest of the questionnaire. The two examples in the box opposite show only some of the items from questions which included a much longer list.

```
┌────────────────────────────────────────────────────────────────┐
│                     Attitudes to working                         │
│                                                                  │
│  PLEASE CIRCLE THE NUMBER UNDER THE HEADING THAT APPLIES         │
│                                                                  │
│                                   Definitely   Partly    Not     │
│                                   True         True      True    │
│                                                                  │
│  1.  Working makes me feel I'm doing                             │
│      something useful ................    ... 1 .......... 2 ...... 3 │
│                                                                  │
│  2.  I never have enough time for everything ... 1 .......... 2 ...... 3 │
│                                                                  │
│  3.  I like the stimulation of going out                        │
│      to work .........................    ... 1 .......... 2 ...... 3 │
│                                                                  │
│  4.  If I lost my job I'd look for another                       │
│      straight away ...................    ... 1 .......... 2 ...... 3 │
│                                                                  │
│                          How I feel                              │
│                                                                  │
│  Exhausted and tired out    □ □ □ □ □   Full of energy           │
│                                                                  │
│  No worries about the future □ □ □ □ □   Often worried about the │
│                                          future                  │
└────────────────────────────────────────────────────────────────┘
```

So, for example, if the woman always felt full of energy, she would tick the box furthest to the right. If she more often felt full of energy than exhausted and tired out, she would tick the fourth box. If she felt that the occasions when she felt either exhausted or full of energy were equally frequent, she would tick the centre box.

Occasionally surveys are done completely by self completion methods. In these cases you will normally have groups of people to deal with, for example, students or schoolchildren.

Composite questions

If a series of identical questions has to be repeated about several related items, it saves space on the schedule if the questions are arranged as one composite question. In the example shown overleaf we are interested in any occasional additions to pay which the informant may have received. This is elicited by the main question and the dependent question (a). Thereafter the information required at (ii) - (iv) is asked for each payment and recorded in the boxes provided.

IF YES

(a)   What payments of this kind have you had in the last 12 months? ITEMISE BELOW

(i) Description	(ii) What was the **total** amount you received in the last 12 months	(iii) Is this amount			(iv) Did you include any of this payment (Q.9a(ii)) in the amount you gave as your usual pay? (Q.8a, or Q.2 if last time's pay same as usual)		
		before tax?	after tax?	DK	If yes: How much was included?		
					£	p	None included in usual pay
		1	2	3			X
		1	2	3			X
		1	2	3			X

Whatever their form, good questions are as simple and universally comprehensible as it is possible to make them while conveying the required meaning. The meaning and purpose will be obvious in most cases. In others they will be explained in the survey instructions and/or discussed at the briefing. Unless you understand a question you will not be able to ask it in a meaningful way, neither will you be able to judge whether the answer you are given is an adequate one given the purpose of the question.

5 Asking the questions

There are two main purposes for which individual questions are put to informants.

These are to collect facts or to elicit information on *opinions, attitudes* or level of *knowledge.*

Not all questions will fit neatly into these categories although the majority will do so. In particular the borderline between fact and knowledge is not always clear just from the reading of a question. It is also possible for the answer to an attitude question to consist largely of factual information. Only the research officer can reliably say whether a question is designed to be one of fact or opinion. This is because the answers to opinion questions are presented as responses to a particular set of words whereas facts are presented simply as tables.

The distinction between the purposes for which questions are asked is important to you, as an interviewer, because it affects the way in which you handle the question whenever a follow up to the initial answer is necessary. As a general rule questions of opinion, attitude or knowledge are handled in a completely standardised way, whereas those which deal with facts can normally be handled more freely. The reason for this is that there is more risk of an interviewer introducing bias on matters of opinion than of fact.

To enable you to know which techniques are appropriate those questions which need to be handled in a completely standardised way are marked with an asterisk under the question number. Other questions are left unmarked.

General points

There is one basic rule which you should remember and apply to all questions and questionnaires. This is that you should not vary the wording or order of the questions except as permitted by the instructions in this chapter. Changes in either can have unpredictable effects which may not always be obvious to you. Even if you find the wording stilted or if your informant anticipates the question you should ensure that each question is read to your informant in its entirety as printed.

Similarly there are two questions which you must ask yourself every time you get an answer from an informant:

1. Has he understood my question? Is he talking about the right thing? If he is not, you should repeat the question before proceeding.

2. Is his answer clear, explicit, and free of ambiguities? If it is not, you should use a *clarifying* probe.

There is also a third question which you must ask yourself every time the question format allows of more than one answer:

3. Has he any *different* answers to make to the same question? You can only find out by asking and should use an *exploratory* probe.

For every question you will go through these stages at least once and may go through stages two and three more than once.

This is known as *probing* and it is in doing this that your technique should vary according to whether or not the question is asterisked. On both types of question, however, a *clarifying* probe is designed to clear up ambiguities, an *exploratory* probe is designed to elicit additional answers.

Pausing

There are many different ways in which you can probe depending on the type of information which you are trying to obtain. But whatever the question it is always worth remembering that a pause or an expectant glance can be a very effective probe. Often this will be enough to make an informant go on to expand or explain what he has said. On most occasions however you will have to put your probing into words.

Probing on asterisked questions (mainly opinion/attitude/knowledge)

Because of the way in which these questions are used and because there is no single correct answer it is important that your behaviour should not influence the informant in any way.

For this reason if any informant mishears or misunderstands the question, in the sense that he answers off the point or says that he does not understand, you should repeat the question once, exactly as it is written. If no adequate reply is then given, you should make a note of this and move on. If an informant asks you to explain a question of this type, you should say that it means what he thinks it means and again repeat it once as it is written.

Although it may seen unsatisfactory to obtain no answer, collecting opinions which are not genuinely held is never valuable and it is for this reason that we do not wish you to continue repeating the question or to change the wording.

Open questions

In most cases you will be given an answer relevant to the question but you will frequently find that you have to use a clarifying probe because the answer is vague or ambiguous. With the same aim in mind of avoiding influencing informants, there are certain standard phrases which we ask you to use when probing these questions. You will in any case find such phrases useful since it is not easy to think quickly of unbiased phrases to use.

The phrases which you may use as clarifying probes are:

Can you explain that a little more fully?

How do you mean?

In what way?

Of these phrases the first is most widely useful since the others are just a little more specific. Much of the time one of these phrases will stand on its own but occasionally, when an informant has said something lengthy, you may need to quote back at them a part of their reply. The following is an example of the use of clarifying probes.

Q.   What do you think are the attractions for married women in going out to work?

A.   *They enjoy it.*

Probe.   Can you explain that a little more fully?

A.   *They enjoy the company, working with other people instead of being alone at home all day. It's a help too.*

Probe.   In what way is it a help?

A.   *The money's very useful, the cost of living being what it is most families can do with some extra earnings from the wife. And it's nice for a wife to feel independent.*

Probe.   How do you mean independent?

A.   *You don't have to ask your husband for it every time you want to spend some money on yourself.*

In this example the interviewer has used each of the clarifying probes which she is allowed to use. After the first response she used the explain probe without quoting the informant's reply back to her because the reply had been very short. After the second and third answers she did quote back part of the reply to make clear which part of the answer needed clarification.

On this occasion the interviewer has been very lucky because she has been given some *different* answers in response to her clarifying probes as well as having the original answer made clearer. Although this happens quite frequently, in most cases, once any ambiguities had been resolved, she would have had to continue by using an *exploratory* probe to find out whether or not the informant had any additional ideas or opinions. In the example given she would only have had to do this after the final answer shown.

There are two set phrases which we ask you to use as exploratory probes. These are:

Is there anything else?

Are there any other (reasons) (items)?

Sometimes you will be able to use these phrases just as they stand. But on the majority of occasions you will have to refer back to the original question on the schedule. If you do not do this, there is a danger that the informant will relate your 'anything else' to what he has just been telling you about and may in any case have forgotten what the basic question was. It is only where the main question is short and the answer simple that you can afford to say 'anything else' alone.

The form *'Are there any other (reasons) or (items)'* can only be used when the original question has asked for reasons or for some other item, such as, for example, attractions. Thus in the example used to illustrate clarifying probes the correct exploratory probe would be:

Are there any other attractions for married women in going out to work?

Whenever you relate an exploratory probe back to the question, be careful to relate it to the *whole* question rather than just a part.

It is important to remember to use exploratory probes until it is clear that the informant has no further opinions to offer. Normally this will be when he says that he has nothing further to say, but occasionally you will have to stop because your informant is repeating himself or clearly dredging around for something to say just for the sake of answering.

The following is an example of an opinion question showing all the stages of probing.

Q.   What *general* advice would you now give to a young person about when to leave school or what kind of a job to go for?

A.   *I'd tell them to stop on if they can.*

Probe. Can you explain that a little more fully?
(clarifying)

A.   *Well it depends if he can get the job he wants or not.*

Probe. How do you mean?
(clarifying)

A.   *If he's interested in a job, see if he can get it: if not, stop on another year to have another chance or to think again.*

Probe. Is there any other general advice you would now give to a young person about when to leave school or what kind of job to go for?
(exploratory)

A.   *If they must leave school, get a job as quick as they can - 'cos round here the fellow down the road has left school over a year and hasn't got a job yet.*

Probe. How do you mean 'get a job as quick as they can'?
(clarifying)

A.   *Not to be fussy about it. Get a job straight away, get any job, and look around while something better turns up. By this they would have gained experience in working and so on.*

Probe. Any other advice you would now give to a young person about when to leave school or what kind of a job to go for?
(exploratory)

A.   *No, nothing else.*

The importance of probing fully and of using the standard probes given cannot be over-emphasised. You should continue to probe until your informant makes it clear by word or expression that he has nothing else to say. At the same time you must guard against overprobing: if your informant is clearly repeating himself or is unable to express himself more clearly you must stop probing.

Only you can judge the point at which you have probed enough and no set rules can be given. But you should remember that underprobing is a much more common fault than is overprobing.

Closed questions

On closed questions which are marked with an asterisk you may use:

> *either* On the whole
>
> *or*   Which comes nearest.

These should be used when you have an informant who is reluctant to answer within the predetermined categories.

Informant's reactions

Occasionally you will come across an informant who becomes embarrassed or concerned because he is having difficulty in answering your questions. This tends to happen mainly in surveys where there are many opinion or knowledge questions.

In these cases you need to make him feel that your concern is only to hear what he does know or think, that you are not an expert on the subject, and that you are in no way critical of his ignorance. It may be helpful to say that you know that you would find it very difficult to answer questions on the spur of the moment.

On knowledge questions informants may sometimes ask you what the correct answer is. This situation needs to be handled with tact as you should not give your informant the correct answer during the interview. This could possibly bias his response to a later question and could lead to him regarding you as an expert. It is best to say either that you are not sure or do not know yourself (this may well be true) or that you think you may have a note about it which you will look up when you've finished the interview.

When handling an asterisked question you must *never* accept answers from anyone other than your selected informant.

Probing on non-asterisked questions

These questions are nearly always of the type to which there is a correct and precise answer. Your aim is to find out what this answer is.

An informant may not be readily able to provide the answer because he simply does not know it or because he has forgotten it. In these cases your role is to encourage him to think about it or find some document which gives him the information or to help him to remember it. In some cases another member of the household will know and since we are concerned with facts such an answer is acceptable.

On this type of question, if your informant misunderstands what you are asking him, in repeating the question you are allowed to alter its wording. In all cases, however, you should read the question exactly as printed in the first instance; and in altering it thereafter you must be very careful not to alter its meaning in any way or to suggest any answer to him.

Many factual questions are answered very quickly and readily but you must be prepared to probe when necessary. One particular point to watch for is that an informant will give you an imprecise answer simply because he does not realise that you require a very precise one. In these cases when you probe for a more precise answer you will often find that the informant spontaneously gives more precise answers to later questions.

There are a number of general rules to follow when probing for factual information of this type:

1. Always ask for the precise information, the exact sum, figure/date, etc.

2. If it is not given immediately, ask your informant if he can give you the more exact ... (sum/date, etc.).

3. If he cannot do this, ask him to give you an approximate answer or to make an estimate. Make sure that you get this as close as possible by, for example, getting him to narrow down a range if he gives you one or by asking which of two answers he thinks is the closest. Be careful never to assume or suggest that the answer falls at the mid-point of the range which he has given you.

Whenever you accept an answer of this kind you should show an 'E' to the left of it to show that it is an approximation.

Although *'don't know'* (DK) codes often appear on a schedule you should only use these after careful probing to try to get at least an estimate.

The right kind of probe to use on a factual question may depend on the specific question and on the research officer's instructions on the amount of detail he requires in answer to that particular question.

Probing on factual questions is left mainly to your discretion but there are some points to remember:

1. Whenever possible use completely 'open' questions, that is, ones which do not suggest an answer to the informant but ask him to think of the exact amount, exact date, or whatever.

2. You need to avoid the use of leading or negative questions. There are

particular ways in which without care you may find yourself suggesting answers to informants. For example, it would be wrong to say *'You are still at school, aren't you?'*, or *'You're not still at school, are you?'*. The correct question is always *'Are you still at school or not?'*

3. If you would find it helpful to suggest any possibility to your informant, make sure that you mention two or three alternatives rather than one only. For example, you might say *'Was it on a weekday or at the weekend?'* but you should never say *'Was it at the weekend?'* By suggesting only one answer you make it easy for your informant to agree with you rather than try to remember.

4. Avoid implying that your informant may not know the answer by saying, for example, *'You couldn't be more exact could you?'* or *'Can't you remember what ...?'* Even in saying *'Can you remember ...?'*, you have to use an encouraging tone of voice if your informant is not to say he cannot.

5. It can often be helpful to ask your informant if he has any document readily to hand which would give him the answer. Depending on the kind of data you are collecting, a cheque book or a diary or appointment card or a bill could all be helpful. Documents are particularly important in financial surveys.

6. Avoid assuming that you know the exact answer from anything which the informant has said earlier in the interview. In conversation or in answering a different question he is unlikely to have taken the trouble to be very precise and you should therefore be prepared to probe as necessary. At the same time it is helpful if you can remember that he has mentioned this earlier and acknowledge this in asking the question. The easiest way to do this is to say *'I think you did mention this but can I just check ...'*

7. When items have to be totalled from an informant's answers it is sensible for you to check your total with the informant. This can be done by saying *'I make the total ..., does that sound right to you or not?'* You should not ask the informant to go through the totalling process himself unless he thinks your answer does not sound right.

8. Be careful not to use phrases that can sound sharp or imply that your informant is inadequate. Thorough but gently worded probes are best to get the information which you want.

9. Questions about past events may give difficulty to informants in remembering the required facts. Sometimes the informant will genuinely not know or not remember and this should be recorded. However there are some techniques that can be used to aid memory recall. The first is to specify clearly exactly which period your question

covers. If, for example, we were interested in jobs held during the previous year, you would make sure that the informant understood that this was, for example, since May 21 last year. It may also help to divide the time into smaller parts and encourage the informant to think about each one separately in order to build up a picture of, for example, jobs held over the whole period. When probing for dates you should always have a calendar to hand and be prepared to work through the relevant time period with your informant. On many surveys involving much historical data some kind of calendar will be issued to help both you and the informant remember and record the necessary detail. Generally it is best to start with the date closest in time to when you are interviewing and work back from there although you must be prepared to be flexible if your informant is tackling it in a different way. Often it will help an informant to remember if you can remind him of a particular point during the period such as Bank Holidays or if you can find out from him whether there were any particular events around the time period, such as a birthday. If you can establish with him any kind of memorable date it is often fairly easy for him to remember whether the date for which you are asking was before or after this. Probing for such things as weekdays or weekends, early or late in the month, summer or winter are all very helpful in establishing dates. Which ones are appropriate will depend on the timescale of your question.

10. On factual data, although you need to guard against overprobing, underprobing is the much more common fault and therefore the one which you should take most care to guard against.

11. Answers given in response to factual questions at different points in the schedule should be consistent with one another. If at any time you feel that this is not the case you should reconcile the answers by explaining that you must have misunderstood something and asking to go back over the relevant questions.

Instructions for particular types of questions

All the points made so far are general ones which relate to probing on questions regardless of their layout and style. In addition to these instructions there are some points to be remembered when asking particular types of questions.

Forced choice questions (p 26) and running prompts (p 27)

When asking these types of questions you should read out all the answers or prompts clearly all the way through to the end of the last item. When the question is a running prompt you should also ensure that the pauses between the prompts are of equal length. They should be just long enough to separate the prompts from one another: if they are any longer than this they make it easy for your informant to interrupt you before you have read out all the items.

If at any time an informant does answer before you have finished reading all the prompts, you should say that you would like to read him all the possible answers before he makes a choice. Similarly, if an informant gives you an answer which is unclear or qualified in some way, you should ask 'On the whole which comes nearest?' and repeat the prompts.

A *priority coded prompt* is the only exception to the rule that the full range of answers should be included in the question wording. When asking questions of this type you should make slightly longer pauses between answers and should accept the first answer on the list which applies.

These questions are *always* marked CODE FIRST THAT APPLIES.

Individual prompts (p 28)

The items in the prompt list form a series of individual questions to each of which an answer needs to be obtained before you can move on to the next item. In dealing with these questions you should always read the question in full for the second as well as the first item on the list. Thereafter you may read out the items only, so long as you are sure that your informant has retained the question in his mind. With a lengthy list of items you will usually need to repeat the full question about every third item but you should always be prepared to ask it in full for every item with a slow or rambling informant.

Scaling questions (p 28)

As with individual prompts you should always read the questions in full for the first and second items and thereafter repeat it in full sufficiently often to ensure that your informant retains his grasp of the questions. If the answer categories are printed on a card, you should ensure that your informant chooses his answers from the card. If there is no card, or if your informant is unable to read for any reason, the answers should be treated as a running prompt: in this case it is normally necessary to read out all the possible answers after each item.

The introduction of a series of questions requiring answers chosen from the same scale tends to change the pace of the interview, especially if preceding questions have been ones where you have encouraged the informant to respond fully. With some informants you may have to explain that you realise that you are not allowing them to explain in detail their complete feelings on the subject. In this instance we need an opinion *on the whole;* when an informant's answers to all the questions in a series are considered together they will show the general tendency of his opinion.

Many scaling questions include a category for neutral opinions such as 'neither agree nor disagree' or 'neither true nor false' or a code for no opinion/Don't know.

Sometimes these are included in the list of possible answers presented to the informant, at other times they are codes for the interviewer's use only. Sometimes you will encounter informants who have difficulty in answering within the range of choices given. Since we are interested in an approximation of their views, encourage them to choose by probing in the following way - *So which of these opinions comes nearest to your own on the whole?'*

Composite questions (p 31)

Composite questions vary widely in their content and may include more than one question format within themselves. Each type of question within them should be handled in the usual way. There is, however, one additional and very important instruction which applies to composite questions. This is that *all* answers to the main question should be obtained *before* you ask any of the subsidiaries. The reason for this is that, since the dependent questions ask for additional information about answers given to the main, an informant can omit responses to the main so as to avoid being asked for more detail about them. This can happen, not because he has anything to hide, but simply because he knows the details will be difficult to remember or because he is becoming bored with the interview.

For composite questions the information asked for at the main is often referred to as *primary data* and the instruction 'collect primary data first' will be given.

Self completion questions

The role of the interviewer in dealing with self completion questions is a limited one. You should however be alert for any sign that your informant is having difficulty in understanding what is required of him and be prepared to explain if necessary. You should also try to ensure that he is taking sufficient time to read the questions and not just answering randomly. When he has completed the self completion section you should quickly check that all the items have been dealt with.

Summary

Remember that as an interviewer your job is to ensure that:

1. all applicable questions are asked and answered within their terms of reference;

2. all answers are clear, unambiguous and as complete as you and the informant can make them.

6 Recording the answers

These are some general principles about recording answers which should always be followed:

1. Answers must be recorded accurately and legibly.

2. They must be recorded at the time of the interview.

3. They must be recorded speedily so as not to impede the flow of the interview.

4. They should be recorded in the exact space and format required.

5. They should be recorded only in pencil or in black ink.

There are two main methods of recording answers. Firstly where the interviewer records in words or numbers the answers given to her. Secondly where she rings a code. Codes may appear on the schedule for either open or closed questions.

Recording answers to open questions

In words

Although answers given in words are sometimes very brief, open questions asking about attitudes are those most likely to cause you difficulty in getting the answers down accurately and completely. To ensure that we see the answer exactly as it was given you should record as follows:

1. in longhand: any words abbreviated at the time of interview will have to be written out in full before returning the schedule to HQ;

2. in the first person: that is, exactly as the informant replies;

3. word for word;

4. at the time of interview; and

5. in pencil or black ink only.

In order to achieve this you should begin writing the moment your informant starts to talk. You should use abbreviations as much as necessary and only as a very last resort should you ask your informant to slow down. Try not to probe until you have recorded all that has already been said: a pause while you finish writing will seem natural to your informant. Open questions normally have a considerable amount of space for recording answers but if it proves necessary you should use margins and other blank spaces rather than condense answers; you should, however, always avoid writing across coding columns. If you do have to record part of an answer away from the recording space ensure that the continuation is clearly marked.

When an open question has precodes printed on the questionnaire you should proceed exactly as above until it becomes absolutely clear that the answer you are being given fits into one of the precoded categories. When this happens you should ring the appropriate code and cross out the verbatim which you have already written.

To help coders who do not have the advantage of sitting in on the interview it is helpful to them if you indicate where you have probed open replies. It is enough to make a diagonal mark as you use the probe; and indicate by the use of initials which probe was used:

'/ae' ='Is there anything else?'

'/ae' ='Are there any other (reasons)?' - if appropriate

'/exp' ='Can you explain that a little more fully?'

'/way' ='In what way?'

'/how' ='How do you mean?'

Whenever you have to repeat the question because it has not been understood, indicate this on the schedule as:

'/R'   = Repeat.

If a probe is used and produces nothing, it is useful to us if you indicate this:

'/ae' —

'/exp' —

However, in any stress situation, it is more important that you remember to use the right probe than that you find time to write it in. Certainly do both if you can do so without slowing up the natural speed at which your informant is talking and you are reporting his words.

In figures

Answers to be recorded in this way are most commonly dates or quantities or amounts of money. You may be asked to record them either on a line or in a series of boxes. The use of a line helps the coder find the answer to be coded quickly and easily. The use of boxes enables the information to go from the interviewer to be placed directly on to the computer.

When boxes are provided there will be one box for each digit and only one digit per box should be entered. When the number you are recording in a box has fewer digits than there are boxes you should put as many zeroes as necessary before the number to ensure that all spaces are filled, for example:

£9 would be written   £ | 0 | 0 | 0 | 9 |

	MONTH	YEAR	

January 1965 would be written | 0 | 1 | 6 | 5 |

When recording on lines or in boxes in this way answers which are DK, or estimated, or in a range should always be written to one side of the recording space rather than in it.

Any answers which are estimates rather than precise figures should have an E entered in front of the amount or quantity given.

Recording answers to closed questions

In these cases you only have to ring a code to indicate the correct answer. It is however very easy to miscode when looking at a lengthy list of codes and great care needs to be taken to avoid this.

Most precoded questions require only one answer and you should be careful to ring only one code. If you ring two codes, the answer will be unusable because we in the office will not know which one is the right one. Where there could be uncertainty about how many codes should be ringed, an instruction will be printed beside the precodes.

CODE ONE ONLY   reminds you that only one code is required.

CODE ALL THAT APPLY   tells you that you should, if appropriate, code more than one answer and that you should use ae probes.

Notes

In general the form of the question and the way in which you are asked to record the answers will give us all the information which we require. But from time to time you will come across unusual circumstances or cases which do not seem to fit completely into the framework of questions. When this happens you should make a full note at the question explaining the circumstances and giving as much information as you can. If a range of questions has been affected, it is preferable to attach a separate note to the front of the schedule.

General points

All recording should be clear and easily legible. For this reason we prefer you to cross out errors rather than rub them out. Careless and illegible recording by an interviewer slows down all the checking and coding work carried out in the office.

7 Classification definitions

At each interview you are asked to collect some facts which will describe the person interviewed and, often, the household in which he or she lives. Since for many of these facts the distribution of different answers is known for the population as a whole (from such sources as the Census) this is an important check on the representativeness of the sample. By putting this information together we can say what kind of people and households our survey represents and can see how the experiences, attitudes and behaviour of informants vary according to their personal characteristics and household circumstances. For example, by comparing the answers given by men and women, members of different social groups, or people of different ages we can tell whether their experiences and attitudes differ according to these factors.

On most surveys classification questions are asked either at the beginning or end of the interview. However, on household surveys you will have to use the household definition when making your initial approach to the informants (see p16). On other surveys where sifting or within-household sampling is required you will have to ask the household composition and possibly other items such as age or working status at this stage.

Before beginning to ask classification questions you should always explain briefly to your informant why this information is needed. When you are asking it as part of a sift you should explain that you would like the information so as to decide whether or not you wish to talk to anyone at the address about the survey you are working on.

The classification items for which you will most often be asking informants are:

> the number and relationships of the people who live in their household;
>
> sex   )
> age   )   generally for all members
> marital status)   of the household;
> working status)
>
> occupation and industry; and
>
> income.

In order to standardise information collected and to enable comparisons to be made between surveys we have evolved definitions of all these items. These will not normally be printed on your questionnaires so you must learn them and apply them whenever you collect classification information.

Household composition

This is normally the first classification question which you ask. The aim of the definition is to ensure that all individuals are included at an appropriate address but that no one can be counted at more than one address. The only exceptions to this are individuals who live in institutions. Our survey samples are normally of private households only and whenever institutions are to be included in a sample special procedures are devised.

The definition of a household is:

> 'one person or a group of people who have the accommodation as their *only* or *main* residence'

> AND   (for a group of people)

> either share at least one meal a day

> or   share the living accommodation.

The majority of households are very straightforward and their composition will be established without difficulty. Nevertheless there are two concepts embodied in this definition either or both of which you will have to sort out on occasion. These two concepts are given below together with more detailed information about what is meant by them.

Residence

The first point which you must establish clearly is which people should be treated as resident at the address. Problems arise only in cases where an individual has more than one address. These individuals should be included at the address which he (or your informant) regards as being his *main* residence. The following special rules, however, take priority over your informant's assessment and should always be applied:

1. Adult children, that is, those aged 16 and over who live away from home for purposes of either work or study and come home only for holidays should *not* be included at their parental address.

2. Anyone who has been away from the address *continuously* for 6 months or more should be excluded even if your informant continues to think of it as their main residence.

3. Anyone who has been living continuously at an address for 6 months or more should be *included* at that address even if he has his main residence elsewhere.

4. Any informant at whose address, in this country, you are calling should be included even if the address is a temporary one, for example, while they are searching for permanent accommodation; you should not, however, include anyone who is making a holiday or business visit only and who remains resident abroad.

5. Addresses used only as second homes, that is holiday homes, should never be counted as the main residence.

Examples

Under rule (1) you would *exclude,* amongst other groups, students away at university or college during term time and children aged 16 and over away at boarding school as well as those working away from home on a permanent basis.

Children working away from home in a *temporary* job would however be included in the parental household, as would children under 16 at boarding school.

Under rule (2) you would *exclude,* for example, individuals who have been in hospital or prison for 6 months or more, members of the Forces on long tours of duty and children who have been in care for an extended period.

Under rule (3) you would *include,* for example, a widowed mother who had been staying in her son's or daughter's home for more than 6 months even though she still had her own home and intended to return there.

In all other cases the question of whether or not the address is the main residence should be decided by your informant.

Splitting into households

Once you have established which individuals are resident you will need to decide which should be counted as members of the same household. There are two alternative concepts involved in this although most households will in fact satisfy both criteria.

> In order to form one household a group of people must
> > *either*
> share one meal a day
> > *or*
> share the living accommodation, that is, a living room or sitting room.

1. Sharing at least one meal a day: this should consist of a main meal but does not imply that the household must always sit down to a meal together provided the food is bought and prepared for joint use. Breakfast may be counted as a main meal.

2. Sharing the living accommodation: that is, a living room or sitting room. Accommodation may still be counted as shared where the address does not have a living room which is separate from the kitchen, that is, where the main living room of the accommodation forms part of the same room as the kitchen. Similarly a household can be treated as one if the living room also has to be used as a bedroom.

A group of people should *never* be counted as one household solely on the basis of a shared kitchen and/or bathroom.

Occasionally an individual or a group of people will have both their own living accommodation (that is, living room/bedsitter and kitchen) *and* the use of a communal living room. In such cases priority should be given to having their own accommodation, and they should be treated as separate households. Situations like this arise in, for example, warden assisted housing for the elderly, flatlet houses, or separate granny flats where the parent occasionally also uses the family living room.

In addition to these rules which must be applied there are one or two general points to note:

1. Members of a household need not be related by blood or marriage.

2. Boarders (that is, unrelated individuals paying for food and accommodation) should be included as members of the landlord's household *provided that no more than three boarders are being catered for.* If four or more boarders are catered for, the guests should be excluded and the proprietor's household only interviewed.

3. There are several groups of people who will only rarely stay at an address but who will nevertheless have it as their main residence. Such groups are merchant seamen, fishermen, oil rig workers, children at boarding school and businessmen who are frequently away from home. But remember that for these groups and all others the 6 months rule still applies.

4. To be included in the household an individual must sleep at the address when he is in residence: anyone who sleeps at one address but has all his meals elsewhere must therefore be included at the address where he sleeps.

Collecting household information

When asking for household composition you should always begin by asking 'Who normally lives here?' (in this flat/part of the accommodation). This question should lead to your being told of any individuals who are not always present and you will then be able to establish whether or not they should be treated as resident.

Because there are several situations in which specific rules have priority over the concept of main residence you should never begin by asking informants about main residence or introduce the concept until you are sure that none of the priority rules apply. Its use should be limited to those occasions on which it has become clear that the household includes someone who has two residences and is not covered by the priority rules. When you do find yourself in a situation where there is some doubt you should begin by asking:

'Do any of you have another address apart from ......?'

Remember that only a very small proportion of people have more than one residence. This is why you are asked to apply your judgement rather than ask about additional residences in all cases.

The priority which you will most often have to apply is that which excludes adult children living away from their parental home. Many parents are inclined to include them if they are regularly home for holidays.

When there is any possibility of doubt about the number of households you should check whether or not meals or living accommodation are shared and you should *always* check this where the household is anything other than husband and wife and children under 16.

Remember that you must check both for sharing of meals *AND* for sharing of accommodation before deciding that there is more than one household. The question you should ask to establish this is:

'Do all the people you've told me about share at least one meal a day or share the living accommodation?'

Recording household information

Household composition is normally recorded in a box which also includes such information as sex and age of household members. This box can be laid out in two ways (see opposite). You may be asked to list household members in relation either to your informant (mainly on named person samples) or in relation to the person whom you have identified as HOH. It is important that you are familiar with both forms and can complete either accurately.

Person no	Relationship to HOH	Age	Sex		Marital status				
			M	F	M	Liv tog	S	W	Div/ sep
1	HOH		1	2	1	2	3	4	5
2			1	2	1	2	3	4	5
3			1	2	1	2	3	4	5
4			1	2	1	2	3	4	5
5			1	2	1	2	3	4	5
6			1	2	1	2	3	4	5
7			1	2	1	2	3	4	5
8			1	2	1	2	3	4	5

Person no.	Relationship to informant	HOH ring	Age	Sex		Marital status				
				M	F	M	Liv tog	S	W	Div/ sep
1	Informant	1		1	2	1	2	3	4	5
2		1		1	2	1	2	3	4	5
3		1		1	2	1	2	3	4	5
4		1		1	2	1	2	3	4	5
5		1		1	2	1	2	3	4	5
6		1		1	2	1	2	3	4	5

Head of household

Having identified the members of the household you are then asked to identify one individual as the head of the household. The definition for this is as follows:

> In a household containing only husband, wife and children under 16 (and boarders) the husband is *always the HOH*.

> Similarly, when a couple have been recorded as living together/cohabiting the male partner should be treated as the HOH.

In all situations where there are other relatives in the household or where some or all of the household are unrelated you should ask the following question:

> 'In whose name is the house (flat/accommodation) owned or rented?'

Except that a husband always takes precedence (see previous page) the person named in reply to this question should be recorded as HOH.

Where the accommodation is supplied with a job or provided rent free for some other reason, the person to whom the accommodation is given in this way becomes the HOH.

Occasionally more than one person will have equal claim to be HOH. In these cases the following rules apply:

1. where they are of the same sex the oldest is HOH;

2. where they are of different sexes the male is HOH.

In some cases you will have to apply both rules in turn to establish the HOH.

These rules on deciding who is HOH are necessary because the use of joint heads of household is not practical for analysis purposes. Because of this it is necessary to have consistency in the way in which decisions are made.

Age

Many people if asked their age in a non-specific way will give it at the next birthday if that happens to be close. For this reason you should always use a very precise question:

> 'How old are you now?' or 'What is your age now?'

> 'How old is he/she now?' or 'What is his/her age now?'

Answers should be recorded in complete years. Children under one year old should be shown as 0.

Marital status

All marital status codes should be completed at the time of interview. The question should be asked by reading out the alternatives printed in the household box in the form of a running prompt, 'Are you married, living together as a couple, single, widowed, divorced or separated?' There are three situations in which it can be coded without asking:

1.   If someone has been described during the interview as husband or wife, you should code married without question.

2.   If someone has been clearly described as boyfriend or girlfriend, fiance or fiancee, or partner, they may be coded as living together. If there is **any** doubt in your mind about their relationship you should ask the question.

3.   Children under 16 may be coded as single without question.

In all other cases marital status must be asked. You should also note that 'living together' takes priority over other categories which arise as a result of a previous relationship.

The categories shown here are those which most frequently occur in the household box but sometimes categories may be either combined or extended. This normally affects only the way in which you record the answers, not the way in which you ask the question.

Work and employment information

Employment status

The household box normally includes a set of codes for employment status for all household members; at other times you may be asked to code this elsewhere on the schedule.

The categories used for employment status are as follows:

1.   *Working.* By this we mean being in paid employment, that is, receiving a wage or salary from an employer or being self-employed.

Working is normally divided into two groups:

(a) full-time workers, that is, those who work over 30 hours per week;
(b) part-time workers, that is, those who work any number of hours per week totalling 30 or less.

Casual workers or workers whose hours vary above or below 30 should be coded according to the number of hours worked in the seven days prior to the day of interview. A person who has more than one paid job should be coded according to the total number of hours worked in *all* jobs.

There are two types of employment which should be discounted when deciding on working status:

(a) For school children and students in full-time education, vacation and part-time jobs should be disregarded.

(b) Work for mail order firms should be disregarded if the inform ant orders goods only for herself and her family.

2. *Unemployed.* This is defined as without paid employment (for any number of hours per week) but actively seeking work.

Instructions on how to treat special employment schemes such as the Youth Training Scheme can vary from survey to survey and are therefore included in survey instructions rather than in this hand-book.

3. *Full-time education.* In this category should be included children and students following full-time courses at any type of educational institution, for example, universities, technical colleges and colleges of further education.

Sandwich students (that is, periods of study, interspersed with periods of employment) should be coded as employed if they receive a salary from an employer throughout the year, as students if they receive a salary only during work periods and arrange their employment via their college.

4. *Not working.* This includes housewives, the retired, and anyone else who does not fall into one of the categories above. Au pair girls should be included in this category rather than being counted as in paid employment.

Occupation and industry

On most surveys details of the occupation(s) of the informant and/or of the HOH are collected so that socio-economic grouping of the household can be carried out.

When the data is analysed comparisons can then be made between groups of different social and economic standing: this is required in fields as diverse as health and health care, housing standards or patterns of household expenditure.

The classification of occupation which is in use includes several hundred codes. It is therefore necessary to collect very full and clear information during the interview if this coding is to be done accurately. There are five basic pieces of information which you need to collect:

1.   The job title.

2.   A description of the *main* job activity.

3.   The level of skill.

4.   The level of responsibility.

5.   The industry/trade/ profession.

Job title. To obtain this information you need only ask the question *'What is your job?'* In most cases this will lead to answers such as 'typist', 'civil servant', 'fitter's mate', 'architect',etc. but if necessary you should go on to ask if their job has a title.

You will often find a heading 'job title' printed on your schedule.

Job description. This is needed because jobs with the same title can vary from one organisation to another and because people sometimes use job titles very loosely. Again you will often find a heading 'job description' printed on your schedule.

To obtain the information it is best to ask *'What do you mainly do in your job?'* If you think that your informant may feel that his job title was self-explanatory you may find it helpful to preface this question by saying that you would like to know this because many jobs include a range of duties.

Many job descriptions which sound straightforward are in reality very vague because they can cover a wide range of different work. Examples of such descriptions are 'engineer', 'machinist', 'technician', 'laboratory assistant', 'miner', 'collector', 'civil servant': in all these examples there are a number of different types or specialisations and a wide range of qualifications and skills can be required.

You should always take care to keep job description details clearly separated from the job title.

Level of skill. This is often expressed in terms of qualifications or apprenticeship or training necessary for the job. It is not important however to know whether the informant himself has the qualifications: what matters is whether people employed doing the same sort of work as your informant would normally need to have served an apprenticeship or gained a particular qualification.

A plumber, for example, would be shown as skilled if he had served an apprenticeship but also if he was doing the work of a skilled plumber without having served an apprenticeship. Similarly a non-graduate civil engineer would be coded as a professional engineer if he was doing a job for which a degree was normally necessary.

The one exception to this rule is that in cases where it is not clear whether or not the job is professional you should establish what qualifications the individual himself holds. An example of a job of this type is 'accountant' which can be given as a job description by either a qualified chartered accountant or an accounts clerk or trainee.

A useful question to establish the level of skill is to ask *'Does your job require any special qualifications or training or do you have to serve an apprenticeship for it?'*

Level of responsibility. In the course of describing his job your informant will probably give you some idea of the level of responsibility, if any, involved in it. However quite a lot of detail is required on responsibility levels and specific points need to be covered: the codes for these will often be printed on your schedule.

(a) If the person is self-employed you need to establish whether he has any employees, and if so, how many. By 'employees' is meant only persons who are *not* members of the family living in the same household. Thus the wife of a self-employed builder who was paid to keep his accounts would *not* be considered as his employee.

(b) If the person is an employee you need to establish whether he has managerial or supervisory duties. In many cases the job description will be such that it is clear that no responsibility of either type is held but in all cases of possible doubt you should check. Where such responsibilities are held it is important in your description to distinguish managerial from supervisory. Broadly speaking the primary function of managers is to plan, organise, coordinate and control work and resources on a long term basis: they may directly supervise staff but it is not essential that they do this. The primary function of foremen and supervisors is the immediate day-to-day control of the basic production of work and the supervision of workers carrying out that particular work.

When establishing whether or not someone has responsibilities of this kind you should always begin by asking:

'Do you have any managerial or supervisory responsibilities?'

It is important that your initial question is as general as this although you will often need to probe further to establish whether the responsibilities are managerial or supervisory.

Industry/trade/profession. To enable the industry of your informant to be correctly classified there is only one item of information which you need to collect:

> A full and clear description of the main activity carried out at the informant's place of work.

To obtain this information you should begin by asking *'What is the main thing which the firm you work for makes or does?'*

By 'the firm' is meant only the particular establishment at which the person works. Thus if your informant works for a large multiple organisation you want to know only the activities carried out in the particular factory/office/shop/complex or branch where he works. Make sure however that your informant realises that you are interested in the activities of the establishment *as a whole,* rather than his particular section within it, for example, if he works in the accounts office of an establishment which makes paint brushes the establishment should be recorded as 'making paint brushes'.

The one exception to this rule is that for the Head Office of any firm you should record the type of business of the whole company.

A contract or temporary worker employed by an agency who has spent the whole week with one employer is coded to the industry of that employer. One who has worked for different employers during the week is coded according to the type of work carried out.

In describing the activities of the establishment there are a number of particular points which you must cover.

(a)   If the activity of the establishment is manufacturing, you need to establish both the actual products manufactured and the materials used in the manufacture, for example, plastic, cotton, man-made fibres, wood, steel, etc. The furniture industry is one example where this type of information would be essential.

(b)   If the activity of the establishment is the sale or distribution of products you need to establish both the types of products which are distributed and whether the business is mainly wholesale or retail.

(c)   If the establishment is an office of some sort you should find out as precisely as possible what the office does. The range of possibilities is very wide and you will simply have to find out as much about it as you can.

Handling occupation and industry
Usually you will find many of the items mentioned above shown as headings on questionnaires. This is less likely to be the case with some of

the items (for example, type of material) which only apply to a proportion of informants. In probing occupation and industry it is best to start off with the questions suggested above but in addition to these you can use any further questions and probes which seem useful to you. You should bear in mind however the need to avoid leading questions or suggesting particular categories of work.

There are no hard and fast rules about the order in which you collect occupation and industry information. According to the circumstances it may be preferable to start with either occupation or industry or to move from job title to industry and back to occupation for more detailed probing. You should be careful however to record all items of information under the appropriate heading: it is often best to record in the informant's own words.

Special cases

1.   If you are interviewing someone who has two or more jobs, record the details of the most remunerative job.

2.   If you are interviewing someone who is unemployed, record the details of the most recent job.

3.   If you are interviewing someone who is retired, record the details of the job which he had for most of his working life or the last main job he had before retirement.

You are issued with code books for both occupation and industry and are asked to code at home from the information which you collected.

On virtually all surveys we need information about the income of the informant and the HOH. Sometimes actual amounts from different sources are needed but in many cases it is only necessary to establish the range of amounts within which the income falls. When asking income it is essential to tell your informant what you would like included and excluded from it and the period of time over which he should consider his income.

The following items should be included in income:

1. All wages and salaries.

2. Overtime payments, bonuses, and tips.

3. All earnings and profits from self-employment.

4. Pensions of all kinds.

5. All state benefits from Dept of Employment or DSS, for example, sickness or unemployment benefit.

6. Child Benefit; in a two-parent household treat this as income belonging to the mother of the children.

7. Income from investments, for example, shares, building society accounts, deposit accounts.

8. Rent from property, including lodgers who are not members of the household.

The following items should be excluded from income:

1. Transactions between members of the household, for example, housekeeping money from husband to wife, payments for board and lodging from other members of the household whether or not they are selected.

2. Amounts drawn from savings or capital.

You may be asked to collect income either *gross*, that is, before any deductions have been made or *net*, that is, after all compulsory deductions have been made. If you are collecting net income you should exclude:

1. Income tax deductions.

2. National insurance deductions.

3. Compulsory superannuation contributions.

Note that voluntary deductions from pay for savings or clubs do not count as exclusions and the amounts therefore should be added back into net income.

When income is required within a range a prompt card is provided which shows the different income groups with a letter or number opposite each group. This is to make the question as simple as possible for your informant and to avoid him having to disclose his income when other people are present.

Period of income

As you will see from the example just given, an income question normally provides alternative time periods over which income should be collected. You should point out these different time periods to your informant and ask him to give you his income for the period which is easiest for him. This will probably reflect the frequency with which his main source of income is paid; for the majority of people this will be either weekly or monthly, particularly if you are collecting net income.

Income should always be collected for the most recent income period, that is, for the last week, or the last month, exceptionally for the last year. Parts of income which fall outside the normal period of receipt should be averaged out to give a figure for the week or month: for example, for a monthly salaried person with an annual bonus you should add one twelfth of this annual figure to the monthly salary. Similarly, for income from investments it will often have to be averaged out to give a weekly or monthly figure: these items of income must never be included in the week or month in which they happen to have been paid if they relate to a longer period than this such as 6 or 12 months.

Asking income

When asking an income question you must always make it clear that you want income *from all sources* and also whether you want it gross or net and for what period. A good basic question to ask is:

> *'What was your income last week (or last month) from <u>all</u> sources before/after any compulsory deductions such as income tax and national insurance or superannuation contributions?'*

This is a complicated definition and you should ensure that the informant has properly grasped it. You should then follow up by saying:

> *'I would like you to include ...'* and mention specific items which you know from the rest of the interview that he may have. For a wage earner you would say *'including wages, overtime, bonus and any other income you have'*. To a retired person you might say *'including your state pension and any other pension or income you have'*. To a self-employed person you would say *'including any money you draw out of the business regularly and any profits at the end of the year, as well as any other income you have'*.

One thing to notice in all these examples is that they all finish by saying *'and any other income you have'*. It is always important to remember that you are collecting income from *all* sources. It is also important to convey to informants, particularly when asking for detailed income, that careful thought and possibly some calculation or looking up of documents is required.

Income of HOH

There are one or two particular points to be made about asking the income of HOH:

1. If the HOH has been present during your interview with someone else in the household, you should address the income question directly to him rather than to your informant; remember however to explain why you are asking it.

2. If the HOH is not present, you should ask his income of your informant only if they are in a close relationship. You may ask it if the relationship is as follows: husband, wife, father, mother, son, daughter, brother, sister (by blood, in law, or adoption). You may also ask it in any case where you have coded a couple as living together without marriage. In cases where the relationship is more distant or there is no relationship you should record the question as not asked.

Summary

The classification section of a questionnaire is the one section where the definitions and instructions are common to virtually all surveys and where you cannot expect to find them included in the survey questionnaire or instructions or covered at a briefing. It follows that you need to memorise them from this handbook and familiarise yourself with the detail by checking unusual cases as you come across them in the field.

8   General points about the interview

Interviewer manner

Before beginning the interview you should make sure that your informant is settled. You should yourself sit facing him whenever possible: this
is the most natural arrangement for any conversation and will be best for
your interview. In particular try to avoid either the formality of facing
one another across a table or the unease of having your informant sitting
by your side and reading over your shoulder.

In any normal conversational situation you would look at the person to
whom you were talking and in an interview you need to learn to do this
between reading the questions and recording the answers. Try also to
read the questions in a natural tone and to phrase them in a conversational
way. This will also help you to be aware of your informants reactions to
what you are saying and to the speed of your questioning.

Although your informant has agreed to participate in the survey, you still
need to give him encouragement and attention if his interest and concen-
tration are to be maintained during a lengthy interview. In carrying out
the interview it will seem natural to you to react in some way to at least
some of the answers which you are being given. It will also seem natural
to your informant that you should do this. However you should be
careful to avoid the use of phrases which could convey the idea that you
approve in some way of the answer which you have been given: very
simple phrases like 'good', 'OK', 'fine', can carry this connotation. Instead
you should use phrases which show your appreciation of the effort an
informant has used to answer a question: suitable phrases would be
'Thanks for taking so much trouble over that/thinking that out so care-
fully/looking that up for me'. Alternatively you should use neutral
phrases such as 'I see' or 'I've got that'.

Throughout the interview your aim is to avoid saying anything which
could influence your informant's answers in any way but at the same time
to show enough appreciation and interest to ensure that he makes a
genuine effort to provide accurately the information which you want.

Try not to allow too much digression on the part of the informant between
questions. While it may not always be wise to keep him too rigidly on the
path of the interview, you cannot afford to lose his interest and attention
before the interview is completed by allowing him to digress too much in

the early stages. Remember that you know how many more questions you have to ask, your informant does not. You should also avoid becoming over involved with your informants in any way. If, for example, you are asked for advice, you should explain that our job is to build up an overall national picture and that we are not qualified to advise on individual problems. The only advice we allow you to give is to suggest that an informant contacts his local Citizens Advice Bureau. It is also wise to avoid telling your informants very much about yourself as an individual or discussing your views on any topic with them.

Interviewing with other people present

If the information being collected is purely factual, there is no harm in a third party being present, so long as he is in a close enough relationship to the informant for the informant not to mind giving the information in his presence. On opinion surveys, however, you must take great care to ensure that the informant's answers are influenced as little as possible by anyone else who is present. If a third party interrupts at all, you should explain as tactfully as possible that at the moment you want only the views of the person being interviewed. It is often helpful to remind them of the way in which the sample was chosen or to offer to note down their views afterwards. If, however, your informant answers only by agreeing with a view expressed by the third party, you will have to record the intervention and the informant's response, and add a note about what happened.

Although you must try to control other people present during the interview, you also need to maintain good relations with any of your informant's family or friends who are present and therefore cannot simply ignore them. Anyone coming in during the interview should get a brief explanation from you as to your presence.

On opinion surveys it is often best to interview the informant alone if you can and on some surveys you will be asked specifically to try to arrange this. Since many households have only one living room it is not always easy to do this, but it can often be arranged by asking the informant to suggest a particular time when other people are not at home or suggesting that the interview is done in a kitchen or hallway. When you are trying to see an individual alone you must take care to avoid making other members of the family suspicious about the reason for it. Many people will accept simply an explanation that it will be easier for you and will avoid disturbing them. As a general rule if you initially explain to your informant that you would like to see him alone, he will find the best way to arrange this.

On surveys where you are asked to see people alone, you may be given further guidance at the briefing as to how to do this. Often the subject matter (eg family planning) will be such that the majority of people will readily accept that it is a personal matter.

Pace and tone of questioning

When carrying out an interview you need to keep it progressing at a pace to suit your informant. The speed at which you ask questions should be governed by the speed at which your informant talks and thinks out his answers rather than by your own natural speed. In particular, you should be careful not to speed up your questioning towards the end of a quota when you have become very familiar with the questions. Remember that an informant is always hearing the questions for the first time and that very few people are used to intensive questioning.

Remember to speak clearly and distinctly throughout the interview even if you are having to speak quietly to avoid disturbing someone else in the room. With an informant who is even slightly deaf, you will need to speak loudly throughout the interview or occasionally perhaps to write a question down for him. You should always avoid showing the schedule itself to an informant.

A slight pause while you are writing down an answer will seem natural and is bound to occur sometimes. But though the informant will see that you are writing it is best to avoid making him unduly conscious of this by reading back his replies to him.

Where several topics are covered in an interview, it often helps the flow of the questioning if you can give a preamble when you are introducing a new topic. Without the use of linking phrases your informant may begin to feel that the questions are never-ending or that they are becoming unrelated to whatever you had said the survey was about.

On many surveys you will find that some preambles are printed on the questionnaire. When you are using preambles of your own, you must avoid saying anything that could influence his answers in any way.

Always thank your informant at the end of an interview. Our enquiries are on worthwhile matters but they are voluntary and we are very grateful to members of the public who give up their time to us. Make sure that there is an opportunity for them to ask you further questions about the survey before you leave the house. Our aim is to leave informants and their families happy about the survey and the experience of being interviewed and in a frame of mind where they are likely to be willing to cooperate in any future survey.

At the end of the interview you should ask for their telephone number if they have one in case either you or HQ should need to contact them.

If anyone asks whether they will be called on again, you cannot give a categoric assurance that this will not happen since occasionally the same household does come up again on another survey.

Unusual informant reactions

Very occasionally, you may meet an informant who behaves in a very facetious way or who refuses to answer many of the questions, or whom you suspect of not telling you the truth. As these are all rare, isolated instances, differing very much one from another, we can offer you only limited guidance on them. But if your judgement is that the informant's attitude is such that you are not collecting reliable information you must return the interview (fully or partially completed) to us with full notes about what happened and why you feel unable to accept the data.

If you break off an interview part way through, remember to be very tactful about how you do it so as to avoid angering your informant. It is often best to abbreviate the interview by skipping questions and not probing rather than to terminate it abruptly.

It must be emphasised, however, that such an occurrence is very rare.

Documents

It is important to have your questionnaires, prompt cards, and pencils readily to hand when you enter a house so that you can produce them in an unobtrusive way. But you should carry them in a folder or briefcase and only produce them after an informant has agreed to be interviewed. Many people are unused to large amounts of paper work and you may have to reassure them that, for example, only parts of it may apply to them.

Leaflets

On all surveys we produce leaflets giving a few brief details about the survey and our organisation. Normally these should be left only after the interview has been completed but in cases where informants are keeping records or where you have interviewed some individuals but have others still to see, it may be helpful to leave one after the main interview.

There is also a general leaflet about the work of the division which you may occasionally find helpful to leave with someone.

Schedules

If on any survey an informant asks to see the schedule or asks you to leave it with him, you must refuse. In general it is best to say only that you are not allowed to let him have one but, if necessary, you can go on to explain that a questionnaire is designed to cover many different situations and that it is the Department's policy not to make them available to the public until the survey is published. If he continues to insist you should suggest that he write to the research officer in charge of the survey.

9 The analysis of a survey

Although you do not need to know in detail about the methods used in analysing surveys it is often helpful for you to have some knowledge of them. Occasionally, for example, you will come across an informant who is interested in how the processing is done.

Primary Analysis Branch and *Survey Branch* are responsible for the processing of all completed questionnaires. Primary Analysis Branch (PAB) is responsible for coding, that is, classification of answers, and the correction of errors. Survey Branch, which forms part of the Information Technology (IT) Division of OPCS, takes responsibility for the provision of computing systems and programs to process the surveys.

At a fairly early stage of a survey, discussions take place between these two branches and Research about the most efficient way of dividing processing into manual and computer stages.

In both Primary Analysis Branch and Survey Branch the speed and ease of their work is very much affected by the accuracy and care with which you complete your schedules.

On some surveys completed schedules are sent directly from Field Branch to the Data Preparation section for conversion into machine readable form. On others they are sent first to PAB for coding. The work of PAB at this stage varies from survey to survey but may include the following:

1. Checking a sample of precoded or partly precoded questions to ensure that the questions have gone smoothly in the field, for example, that there have been no problems with definitions and that the informants have been able to answer within the terms of the precodes.

2. When questions are partly precoded those answers which were specified have to be coded unless there are so few of them that this is not considered worthwhile.

3. Checking that key information is present and, so far as can be checked, is correct.

4. The checking of factual information given at different points on the

questionnaire for consistency. In some cases conformity with known external facts is also checked, for example, state benefits such as pensions cannot usually be above certain amounts. This type of checking is particularly important on financial surveys and on those which contain much information about dates.

5. The coding of those parts of the questionnaire where the answers have been recorded in words. This may be done by constructing an appropriate list of codes from a sample of all the answers. This code list is then discussed and agreed with the project manager. Particular categories may be small numerically but of particular interest in the survey.

Many of these checks are now done by computer, leaving PAB to deal with any errors discovered following the edit stage.

The data is keyed into a computer by the Data Preparation section of IT Division. Before this can be done keying instructions must be specified. These instructions tell the operator exactly what has to be keyed and in what order. The maximum space which each response will be allowed to occupy (called the field width) is also defined. Keying instructions are often printed on the schedule but this is done in such a way as not to spoil its clarity for the interviewer.

The speed and accuracy of data preparation depends very largely upon the clarity with which interviewers have recorded numbers and ringed codes. In order to be regarded as proficient, operators are expected to key at an average of 13,000 key depressions per hour.

The purpose of editing is to attempt to correct any inconsistencies in the data which may have arisen at earlier stages. Each data item is checked for valid type (essentially whether it is alphabetic or numeric information) and range (that is, does it fall within pre-specified limits). Edit checks are also carried out on the continuity and consistency of the schedule data. Continuity checking seeks to ensure that the correct pathway has been followed through the interview. Consistency checks are specific to the subject matter of the interview and typically involve cross-checking responses from one part of the schedule with another part. Occasionally introduction of facts external to the interview is involved, for example, conditions for receipt of certain state benefits. Diagnostic messages are produced for any cases which fail the checks.

Error reports are passed to PAB for scrutiny. Sometimes corrective action can be decided upon merely by consideration of the printout, sometimes the actual schedules have to be consulted. The edit for any particular survey may contain literally hundreds of error checks. A specially tailored edit program has to be constructed for each new survey to reflect the detailed logic of the interview.

The bulk of the analysis done on survey data involves the production of frequency tables of varying degrees of complexity. However, not all items of information collected in the interview are suitable for tabulation without further modification. For example, numerical data such as ages, sums of money, etc. usually have to be grouped into bands. Often information from several questions is combined into a single item of data, for example, income from different sources is used to give total income or the income of different individuals is combined to give household income.

Reporting on the survey

One of the main responsibilities of the research officer for a survey is presenting the findings to the Commissioning Department.

Tables of results are often sent to clients as they become available and any issues which they raise are discussed at this point. Occasionally the delivery of tables is the only commitment which SSD has made.

In some cases an edited tape is sent to client departments who may then publish selected results themselves, often in conjunction with other material which they already have. In these cases SSD normally produces a technical report giving details of the methods used in collecting and analysing the data.

For the majority of surveys, however, a full interpretive report of the findings is published by HMSO or OPCS so that the survey results become widely available. Publication is only undertaken with the agreement of the client.

Published reports on completed surveys are sold either through HMSO bookshops or by OPCS and are often available in libraries.

Index

Printed in the United Kingdom for HMSO
C25 8/91